To Phil, my faithful sounding board and brilliant collaborative mind. Your talents impact more lives than you know. Thank you for being my consistent true north and a champion of our everyday God!

CONTE

Dedication
Introduction
49 Pictures 1
Absurd Obedience 3
A Little More Like Jesus 5
Be Like Mark 7
Come Away and Rest for a While 9
Confessions From a Former Battering Ram 11
Cry Out 13
Dealing with a Bully 15
Don't be Shackled by Someone Else's Chain 17
Feel Like You've Lost Your Spiritual Sparkle? 19
Getting Beyond the Why 21
How to Anchor Your Heart While Raising Your Children 23
How to Bottleneck a Blessing 25
Is That Grass Really Greener? 27
Keep Your Eyes on Jesus 29
Letting Go Doesn't Equal Abandonment 31
Living Abundantly 33
My Shame Is Gone 35
No Looking Back 37
Not By Bread Alone 39
Not Taking Myself Too Seriously 41

Participation Required	43
Relationship > Religion	45
Seeing Pieces of His Heart	47
Soaring like a...Turkey	49
Sometimes Love isn't Convenient	51
Stop the Bleed	53
The Act of Imitating	55
The Price of Friendship	57
Trash Bags of Teddy Bears	59
Unsanitized Prayers	61
Victorious Chipping	63
Walking Each Other Home	65
Wear Your Own Armor	67
When a SEAL Taught Me About Care	69
When I Least Expected It	71
White Space	73
Workouts with Hershey	75
Worship 24/7	77
You Are Not Alone	80
About The Author	83

INTRODUCTION

Hello there, friend!

I have always appreciated reading other people's God stories. Real life accounts of how God showed up in their everyday moments to be with them. Maybe it was to help, perhaps it was to comfort, but it was always to reveal Himself in a way in which the person got to know Him just a little bit better.

The pages that follow are just that – everyday stories that God used to help me get to know Him just a little bit better.

I pray they make you smile (maybe even giggle at times), ponder, and reflect upon your own experiences to consider the many times God has intersected your everyday life. He's always present. We just don't tend to always remember that.

So, grab a cup of coffee, nestle in to that comfy chair, and take a deep breath with me as we spend a few minutes talking about how amazing it is that our God is an everyday God!

May you be inspired!

Kristen

49 PICTURES

How do you consolidate a person's life into a mere 49 pictures?

That's the question I was asking myself after my mother passed from this life into eternity.

My dad, brother, and I had flipped through an assortment of old photo albums in an effort to find the perfect pictures that told the story of my mother's 75-years of life that could be used in a video montage for her funeral.

We spent hours looking at images of my mom as a young child, a graduate, a bride, a new mom, a teacher, a quilter, and a grandmother to name just a few.

"There is an occasion for everything, and a time for every activity under heaven..." (Ecclesiastes 3:1 HCSB)

That verse had never been as meaningful to me until I sat there surrounded by hundreds of pictures that testified to this Biblical truth.

"...a time to give birth and a time to die...a time to weep and a time to laugh; a time to mourn and a time to dance; a time to embrace and a time to avoid embracing...a time to tear and a time to sew; a time to love and a time to hate; a time for war and a time for peace." (vs. 2-8)

Each picture revealed a "time to" moment in her life. Each smile, event, or activity had been meaningful to her. There was a story attached to every photograph. It was painfully difficult trying to whittle down hundreds of images to just a few that best highlighted her life.

In the end, we wound up with 49 pictures that we felt best summed up my mom. But in reality, she was so much more than those images could aptly convey.

Aren't we all? How can any of us feasibly condense our lives or anyone else's into a few photographic prints?

Obviously, we can't. From birth to death, the breadth and depth of our lives are walked out in the accumulated seconds and minutes that make up the time we have been gifted on this earth.

Ephesians 5:16 exhorts us to, "*...make the most of our time...*"

Pictures can only capture moments. They're not comprehensive of one's life. Only God holds that ability – the ability to see our lives from beginning to end and help us make the most of it.

Robin Williams' character John Keating in the classic film *Dead Poet's Society* spoke to the very heart of this when he said, **"Carpe diem! Seize the day...make your lives extraordinary!"**

Reflective Question: How can I make my life extraordinary today?

ABSURD OBEDIENCE

It didn't make any sense of those who had a front row seat to my life.

I only wanted one thing as I was walking through my divorce years ago – well, two actually – my children.

Throughout the court process, I didn't fight for alimony. I wasn't arguing about property and assets. I wasn't concerned about who got what.

I voluntarily laid it all down in exchange for my young daughter and son.

It was my step of obedience that I believed God was asking of me. I knew He would honor it and I had no question that He would take care of us and provide for us in the future.

However, my choice looked insane to people around me. They didn't quite understand my thought process. My decision looked weak and absurd. I became the target of furtive glances and whispered remarks.

I wasn't the first person to obey God in a way that seemed bizarre to others.

The Bible is loaded with outlandish obedience stories.

Genesis 22 holds one that, if scripted for a movie today, would probably sweep the Academy Awards for its intense plot, heart pounding drama, and riveting characters.

God instructed Abraham to, *"Take your son, your only son Isaac, whom you love...and offer him as a burnt offering..."* (Genesis 22:1-2 HCSB)

The following 17 verses detail Abraham's unquestioning (but not necessarily *easy*) obedience as he saddles his donkey, grabs a couple servants, his son Isaac, a bundle of wood and heads up a mountain to execute this sacrifice – his beloved son.

(Honestly, can you imagine what must have been going through Isaac's mind as his father was tying him up and putting him on top an altar of wood?!)

According to the story, Abraham raised the knife and at the last minute, God intervened and provided a ram to be sacrificed instead.

Have you ever had moments where your obedience to God looks absurd? It may not be as extreme as Abraham's, but those around you may still question your actions because they just don't understand them?

Each of our paths are unique. No one else walks the journey mapped out for us. Only we do and, as a result, only we really know what our specific steps of obedience might look like with God.

But know this – in whatever way God is asking you to be obedient right now, *He will provide*. He was faithful to Abraham; He was faithful to a young, single mom so many years ago; He will absolutely be faithful to you, too.

"*My God will supply all your needs...*" (Philippians 4:19 HCSB)

> *Reflective Prayer: Father, help me obey You today no matter how absurd it may appear to others. Amen.*

A LITTLE MORE LIKE JESUS

My husband and I decided to redo our living room.

It was a complete overhaul. We got rid of every bit of furniture, décor, and curtains. We patched cracks in the walls, put up a fresh coat of paint, and deep-cleaned the carpets.

It was no small undertaking. For months, the room sat totally empty while we waited for our new furniture to arrive.

During that time, it didn't look much like a living room at all.

But then, pieces of furniture began to come in. Bit by bit, wall décor and room accents were added. And slowly, one simple day at a time, it began to look and feel more like a living room.

Throughout this extensive process, God reminded me of something I pray every day.

"Lord, please help me look a little more like Jesus today."

Just like I did with my living room, God did a complete overhaul on me when I first decided to give Him my heart years ago.

While my decision to follow Jesus was sincere, there was still a lot of the old Kristen that God needed to sort through, remove, and utterly discard.

Slowly, He transformed me into the new Kristen one day at a time.

He adorned me with new habits that reflect His heart, thoughts that more readily line up with His word, and a deep desire to see Him glorified in all that I do and say.

Now, three plus decades after my original decision to become His, His work continues in me. One simple day at a time.

"Lord, please help me look a little more like Jesus today."

We are all remodeling projects of God's. Regardless of what stage of development you're in, as the Master Builder, Creator, and Designer, He is dedicated and passionate about making you look more like His Son every day.

2 Corinthians 5:17 tells us, *"...that anyone who belongs to Christ has become a new person. The old life is gone; a new life has begun!"* (NLT)

Once you decide to exchange your old life for a new one, the adorning, transforming, and beautifying work will continue for the rest of your life! One simple day at a time.

> *Reflective Question: Where is God helping me look a little more like Him today?*

BE LIKE MARK

I have a friend named Mark. Mark has stage 4 metastatic breast cancer.

This is the third time in his young 48-year old life that he has wrestled with some form of cancer.

But, here's the thing. Mark is, hands down, the most inspiring person I know.

He lives in the moment.

His joy is overflowing.

His outlook is positive.

His words are full of hope.

He purposefully uses every minute.

He understands he's terminal. But, more importantly, he understands we *all* are terminal.

From the time we are born, the countdown begins. Our days are numbered (Job 14:5; Psalm 139:16) and our life is like a vapor (James 4:14; Psalm 144:4).

Most of us don't want to think about that and we certainly don't want to talk about it.

Not Mark.

He walks in the undeniable truth that to live is Christ, but to die is gain (Philippians 1:21).

Mark has a clear and deep understanding of his purpose. His life is ablaze with one mission – to love his Maker, his Best Friend, and King with every minute he's been gifted and to tell as many other "terminals" about Jesus.

Mark knows that this diagnosis is not the end. It's temporary. It's earthly.

He has complete confidence in the certainty that Heaven will bring fullness of healing, joy unspeakable, and eternal fellowship with his God.

That is his hope and future and, because of that, Mark walks out his temporary existence knowing his eternal future is secure.

Mark has no clue when God will call him home. Do any of us?

In the meantime, God encourages all of us to make the most of our time and to redeem it (Ephesians 5:16).

Temporary pain can't stop us. Physical discomfort can't stop us. Dismal circumstances can't stop us.

We serve a God who endured all of those things and so much more in order to have fellowship with us, so that we could spend forever with Him.

Reflective Question: How can I live with this kind of eternal passion today?

COME AWAY AND REST FOR A WHILE

A quiet day!

I threw on some comfy clothes, turned off my phone, queued up several of my favorite movies, and grabbed my snacks and coffee.

I had just come through weeks of non-stop activities, people, and work. While I enjoyed every minute of it in the moment, I could feel my soul tugging for some quiet as the stream of busy days unfolded.

Time to just be alone. Time to stare out the window, watch a good movie, or just sit in my rocking chair and give myself space to think.

Time to recharge, refill, and refresh.

We all need those, don't we? Even if we don't like to admit it!

Life can be crazy! We book our calendars into the margins, run ourselves ragged with activities and appointments, and generally overextend our finite energy only to find that at the end of each day we fall into bed exhausted.

Stretched beyond our healthy limits, we try to do it all. The unfortunate truth is that this stretching, trying, running, and doing will eventually catch up with us and we'll find our internal tanks drained dry and our souls running on fumes.

We all need quiet space.

This well-known, ancient truth is even written about in the Bible.

Jesus and His disciples were neck-deep in a season of ministry in which the word "busy" doesn't even come close to defining. Mobs of people were following Him as He made His way through the region healing the sick, feeding the hungry, and teaching the masses.

Yet, during one of the most hectic times of this intensely demanding season, Jesus looked at His disciples and said this incredible statement, *"Come away by yourselves to a remote place and rest for a while."* (Mark 6:31 HCSB)

The most highly sought after man on the planet at that time clearly understood the need for quiet.

What does that look like for you? Perhaps, it's an hour soaking in a bubble bath. Maybe, it's having someone else watch the kids so you can just take a drive and listen to your favorite music.

Regardless of what it uniquely looks like for you, I urge you to carve out the quiet space that your heart and mind so desperately need right now.

Refill your tank. Refresh your soul. Rest for a while.

> *Reflective Question: What is something I can do this week that helps me rest?*

CONFESSIONS FROM A FORMER BATTERING RAM

I have a confession.

There was a time in my life when I aggressively tried to shove Bible verses down people's throats in an effort to bring them to Jesus.

It didn't work out very well (*imagine that*) and I didn't have a large circle of friends (*go figure*).

But in my passion for wanting others to "see the truth" I felt compelled to be this zealous.

This zeal was magnified with the pressure that somehow it fell to me to *make people* agree with "the truth" before parting ways.

It took years of God chipping away at that very distorted mindset to help me see that He doesn't treat people like that. Why should I?

The Holy Spirit never shows up at the door of our hearts with a battering ram.

He's a gentleman. He knocks. If we don't answer, He goes away and waits for another opportunity to knock again.

"Behold, I stand at the door and knock. If anyone hears my voice and opens the door, I will come in…" (Rev. 3:20 NKJV)

So gracious. So thoughtful. So polite.

No spiritual wrecking ball tactics. No breaking down the door. Just courtesy, respect, kindness, and patience.

Jesus modeled it beautifully.

We don't read about Him feeding the hungry, healing the sick, and teaching the attentive crowds while trying to ramrod His divine insights into their heads.

More than that, there's no record of panic, surprise, or shock as He spoke such life-giving words to people who chose not to listen to Him in the moment.

He just spoke truth. The Holy Spirit knocked.

What the listener did with that truth was between them and God.

That's an invaluable lesson that anyone who professes to be a Christ-follower should hold close to their hearts.

We can't – and don't – save anyone.

We simply share the truth. The Holy Spirit does the knocking. God does the saving.

> *Reflective Question: How can I partner with God today as I trust Him to save those around me?*

CRY OUT

As a young mother, the incident embarrassed me to no end.

My 3-year old daughter and I had run to the grocery store for a few things. Upon arrival, I had placed her in the front seat of the shopping cart so I could keep an eye on her.

After gathering the items on my list, we headed for the check-out line.

It was a small mom and pop's store. They didn't have a big intercom system. If the cashier needed help bagging the customer's groceries, they would just yell for help and the nearest bag boy would come running.

My young daughter had seen this action displayed numerous times as we shopped there often.

On this particular occasion, my little one thought she'd preempt the cashier. As I pushed our cart up to the conveyor belt and began placing my items on it, my daughter yelled the magic words as loud as she could, "*SACK UP!*"

Then, she sat there and excitedly watched for someone to answer that call.

I wish I could say that I did, too, but every fiber of my being was mortified as I quickly hushed my little girl, smiled sheepishly at the cashier, and kept my head down hoping to get out of the store without my offspring popping off with any more outbursts.

It wasn't until after my embarrassment wore off that I realized how much her example was worth following.

My young daughter had given me a poignant show and tell example of how to cry out, lift up my voice, and yell for help – something the Scriptures encourage us all to do.

"This poor man cried out, and the Lord heard him, and saved him out of all his troubles." (Psalm 34:6 NKJV)

"I cried out to the Lord…and was delivered from my enemies." (Psalm 18:3 ISV)

Cry out is just another way of saying yell. We open our mouths, yell, and God comes running!

The Bible is full of stories of people crying out – in praise, in desperation, in need, in trouble. God welcomes it all!

More reliable than the fastest bag boy, His Word promises He'll come running if we go ahead and cry out!

"…everyone who calls on the name of the Lord will be saved." (Romans 10:13 HCSB)

> *Reflective Question: What is burdening me today that I just need to cry out to God about?*

DEALING WITH A BULLY

I hit the crash bar on the door of the middle school and went running across the street. Finding sanctuary in a public laundromat, I called my Dad and asked him to come pick me up.

A bully had it out for me. To this day I'm not really sure why. At the ripe old age of 13, I aimed to be as well-liked by everyone as I possibly could, but this specific kid just wasn't having it.

That particular night, as I sat with a handful of classmates watching a middle school basketball game, this girl spread the message that she was going to "beat me up." The moment I saw her heading my way, I bolted.

I huddled between the washing machines churning through their cycles until my Dad arrived to rescue me.

I don't know if that girl even followed me to the *King Koin Laundromat* that night. All I know was that her threat alone sent me running.

I have felt that way countless times with my spiritual adversary, as well. Have you?

The devil and his devious cohorts use these tried and true bullying tactics all the time and are highly skilled at it.

They spew threats, throw taunts, and lie in an effort to get us on the run - cowering in fear and cringing with worry as they slowly and methodically look to tear apart our faith.

2 Corinthians 2:11 encourages us not to be *"...ignorant of (the enemy's) schemes."* Bullying is one of the devil's most classic schemes and, to be clear, it's really all he has.

But, here's the beautiful truth that, when seen clearly, will enable you to stand toe to toe with any spiritual bully – *everything they say is a lie.*

Paul tells us to, *"...take captive every thought to make it obedient to Christ (2 Cor. 10:5)."* Why? Because our minds (our thoughts) are where the war is waged. The devil knows he can't strong-arm us into doing anything we don't want to do.

But, he has seen over the years how highly effective spouting lies and hurling threats can be and, when bullies find a hot button to push, they don't tend to change their tactics.

The solution? Examine those taunts and threats as you hear them in your mind and replace them with what's true. Find those incredible verses that apply to your circumstances and pray them over your life, your heart, and your mind.

In doing so, you'll turn the tables on those bullies and put them on the run!

(Of course, calling your Daddy always helps, too!)

> *Reflective Question: What thoughts do I need to take captive today and give to God?*

DON'T BE SHACKLED BY SOMEONE ELSE'S CHAIN

Turn your radio dial to any contemporary Christian station these days and you'll hear plenty of songs about chains and how God is a chain-breaker.

As we sing those songs, we tend to envision the personal chains that God has broken from our own lives – addictions, habits, and strongholds.

But how often do we consider the impact of other people's chains on us?

Living in a broken world, we are all subject to "chains" – toxic tendencies, wrong thinking, and generational shackles that get passed down to us. Invisible to the naked eye, the ramifications of these chains impact our thinking, decisions, and actions.

But, they also have a ripple effect on those around us.

Many times, we get frustrated at our spouses, our parents, and our closest friends for not loving us, leading us, or supporting us well, all the while not taking into consideration the chains they have in their own lives.

My first marriage was a perfect example of this as I anticipated, expected, and waited on my husband to love and encourage me the way I thought he should. Yet, the further into our marriage we got, the more my hopes and expectations were dashed as what I longed for versus what I received were two totally different things.

I was discouraged more times than I can count and heartbroken more days than I care to admit as my faith seemed shackled to the way I was being treated. Yet, the simple truth was my husband never had his chains broken.

I was waiting on him to walk in a freedom he didn't know.

The result was that I was growing stagnant and unfruitful in my own walk with God as I hitched my hopes to a person still wrestling with their own fetters. It required God opening my eyes and helping me see that no one can hinder my growth, my progress, or my obedience to Him except me.

Every person we lock eyes with today has their own chains. But, here's a lifesaving piece of advice - *don't let anyone else's chains keep you from being faithful.*

God has called us to be light-bearers, salt-shakers, and ambassadors on mission for His Kingdom. Part of that high calling is to walk in freedom ourselves so that we can, in turn, help others find freedom from their chains as we introduce them to the only Chain-Breaker, Jesus.

"The Spirit of the Lord is on me, because He has anointed me to preach good news to the poor, He has sent me to proclaim freedom to the prisoners (those in chains) and recovery of sight for the blind, to set the oppressed free..." (Luke 4:18 NKJV)

> *Reflective Question: Are someone else's chains keeping me from being fruitful today?*

FEEL LIKE YOU'VE LOST YOUR SPIRITUAL SPARKLE?

Do you ever feel like you've lost your spiritual sparkle?

I sure have!

Simply walking through a typical day can remove our shine quickly as we navigate everything from fractured relationships to on-the-job stress.

But God, who sees our circumstances from a much higher vantage point, always has a purpose. He always has a plan. We may not see it in the moment, but it remains true nonetheless.

Genesis tells the story of Joseph, a boy from a large family who happened to be his father's favorite. Joseph's story has enough sparkle remover moments to help any of us see our bad days through a different lens!

First, his jealous brothers schemed to kill him, but opted to throw him in a pit instead (Gen. 37:24).

Then, they sold him to a group of traveling slave-traders (Gen. 37:28).

Then, he was brought to Egypt and sold to Potiphar, a guard captain of Pharaoh's (Gen. 37:36).

Then, after settling in there, Potiphar's flirty wife makes a move on him and accuses *Joseph* of wrong (Gen. 39:16-18)!

THEN, Potiphar believes his lying wife and tosses Joseph in prison (Gen. 39:19-20)!

Just enduring a series of events like that would wipe most of our spiritual sparkle clean off us, wouldn't it?

Yet, here's what I love most about Joseph's story and his example –

his eternal perspective.

By the time his story comes full circle, he makes this statement to his remorseful brothers, *"...you planned evil against me; God planned it for good..."* (Gen. 50:19-20)

Joseph understood Who was ultimately in charge. Consequently, no pit or prison, no false accusation or relational dysfunction was able to take his spiritual sparkle away.

He knew God had a plan and, while I'm sure he didn't necessarily see it perfectly while staring at the walls of a pit or the inner room of a prison, he never stopped trusting.

God planned it for good.

Has the weight of the world or difficulties with people caused you to lose your luster? Do you feel like your spiritual sparkle is tarnished beyond hope?

Look up, my friend! Shift your vantage point from earthly to eternal and know that whatever you're going through today, *God has planned it for good*!

> *Reflective Prayer: Father, I trust that everything happening in my life right now has eternal purpose. I give you my heart and my life today and believe that You have planned everything I go through for good. Amen.*

GETTING BEYOND THE WHY

Have you ever felt like you just can't get a grip on all the *why* questions racing through your mind?

Me too.

Why did God allow me to go through a divorce?

Why would God permit my child to run away and become prodigal?

Why did my mom suffer so long with Alzheimer's?

Those are just a few of mine.

We all deal with *why* questions in life. Questions that we can't answer and are beyond the scope of our finite understanding. Questions that, if left unchecked, can erode the foundations of our faith and have us turning our backs on God.

The book of Judges tells the story of a young man who had *why* questions, too, and reveals God's wise and empowering response.

Israel had prospered and enjoyed peace for nearly half a century under the leadership of Deborah, prophetess and judge. This peaceful season came to an end as the Israelites *"did what was evil in the sight of the Lord."* (Judges 6:1)

As a result, Israel opened themselves up for oppression, marauding, and pillaging at the hands of several enemy tribes.

The Lord approached Gideon with an invitation - help deliver Israel from the grasp of Midian (the enemy they happened to be up against at that time).

But instead of excitedly jumping at this opportunity, Gideon responded with an anguished *why*.

"...why has all this happened? Where are all the wonders that our

fathers told us about?...the Lord has abandoned us." (Judges 6:13)

His heart was broken over the oppression of his people and he was looking for answers.

God's response is not what most of us would expect.

"Go in the strength you have...I am sending you...I will be with you." (Judges 6:14 & 16)

God didn't even address the *why*! Not because He was heartless and didn't care, but because He knew it was in Gideon's best interest to move on and look ahead.

Clearly, it wasn't necessary for God to expound on all the behind-the-scenes details. What got the Israelites into this pickle in the first place wasn't the point.

Gideon trusting God in the present was the point.

There are countless things in this life that we'll never fully understand. Spinning our wheels, blaming God, and getting hung up on the *why* is a colossal waste of time.

It will always be true that, this side of Heaven, *"We don't yet see things clearly. We're squinting in a fog, peering through a mist..."* (I Cor. 13:12 MSG)

That's part of being human. We won't know everything; we don't have all the answers.

But God does and that's enough.

> *Reflective Question: Are there any "why's" I need to surrender to God today so I can move forward in my divine calling?*

HOW TO ANCHOR YOUR HEART WHILE RAISING YOUR CHILDREN

Do you have children? If so, you'll understand there is no greater joy, challenge, or delight than that of being a parent.

From the time they are born, the stewardship of parenting begins.

And while the first year deprives more parents of sleep than military boot camp, the ability to protect and shelter those newborns from all the pitfalls of the world are pretty easy.

But then they grow and with each passing year, they learn, absorb, and react to the environments around them – outside of the home and in.

It can be scary, disheartening, emotionally draining, and unnerving as you walk with them through the ups and downs of growing up.

Navigating everything from bad words to broken hearts can be exhausting.

Parents need a safe place. A place to anchor their hearts and souls when those daunting moments arise and it feels like your parenting world is spinning out of control.

In the midst of raising my four children, I quickly realized the crucial need to keep God's promises in front of my eyes (sticky notes all over the place helped) so that my heart didn't faint whenever we hit one of life's speed bumps (and there were many).

Here were a few of my favorites that I prayed often and spoke out loud frequently:

"A righteous person acts with integrity; his children who come after him will be happy." (Proverbs 20:7 HCSB)

"They will not labor without success or bear children destined for

disaster, for they will be...blessed by the Lord along with their descendants." (Isaiah 65:23 HCSB)

"All your children will be taught by the Lord; great will be the peace of your children." (Isaiah 54:13 NAB)

To be clear, not every day looked (or felt) like my children would be happy, blessed, or peaceful (like these promises stated). Quite the contrary!

There were many days, months, and even years when I questioned if I'd ever see these promises come to pass in the lives of my kids.

But that's where faith comes in, doesn't it? Or sometimes just plain hope.

The beauty of God's promises is that *He* brings them to pass. Not us. *He* does the work in the hearts of our kids. Not us.

He gives us His promises so that we can bind our hearts to what's sure and eternal, not what's fleeting and temporary.

We just grab hold of His Word, pray, and trust the He loves our kids even more than we do.

> *Reflective Prayer: Father, thank You for loving my kids even more than I do! Thank You for Your precious promises that help anchor my heart in Your word as You do the eternal work in theirs. Amen.*

HOW TO BOTTLENECK A BLESSING

If you've ever taken a road trip with children, then I'm certain you're quite familiar with the question that gets asked countless times while traveling, *"Are we there yet?"*

Sometimes it's asked as a genuine question of curiosity. Other times the question's laced with a surly attitude – which can delay the journey further as you pause to deal with the attitude.

The latter is what Moses continually had to navigate as he led the children of Israel through the wilderness.

A journey that by all geographical calculations and historical accounts should have only taken 11 days was stretched over a period of 40 years! (Deut. 1:2)

Why?

Because the Israelites wouldn't quit grumbling, complaining, and fussing as they tried, time and time again, to do things their way instead of trusting the Divine Planner of the trip.

God reached His tipping point with their unbelief and vowed that the adults who had been supernaturally delivered from slavery in Egypt would never enter the promised land.

He told Moses to tell them, *"I have heard the Israelites' complaints that they make against me...[they] will die in the wilderness...I swear that none of [them] will enter the land I promised to settle [them] in...I will bring [their] children...into the land...and they will enjoy it."* (Numbers 14:26-31)

The book of Joshua says it this way, *"The Israelites wandered in the wilderness forty years, until all the nation's men of war who had come out of Egypt had died, since they had not obeyed the Lord."* (Joshua 5:6)

Hindsight being 20/20, it's easy to read the Israelite's story and judge them harshly because of their blatant propensity to grumble, complain, and rebel.

Can't they see that their fussy attitude is delaying their journey?

Don't they know that their continual rebellion is blocking God's intended blessing for them?

But, they didn't…and, it cost them.

How many times have we prevented God's blessing in our lives by clogging the pipeline with complaints?

How often do we delay or add layers of detours to our journey because of suspicion and mistrust towards God?

Oh, that we would learn from the children of Israel's story and continually root complaining out of our lives so that God's blessing would flow freely to and through us!

Reflective Prayer: Father, please help me "Do everything without grumbling or arguing, so that (I) may be blameless and pure, (a child) of God who (is) faultless in a crooked and perverted generation, among whom (I) shine like (a star) in the world." (Phil. 2:14-16)

IS THAT GRASS REALLY GREENER?

My husband and I jumped in our car and journeyed off on a cross-country road trip that took us from Georgia to Montana and back again.

We were like kids in a candy store as we started off. We turned on some tunes, starting munching on some of our snacks, and chattered away as we eagerly absorbed the scenery passing by.

We didn't have an itinerary. We were winging it and our minds were racing with all the things we hoped to see and do!

But it became very obvious early in our trip that we were *not* going to be able to see or do everything we really wanted.

Our time was limited and our energy was finite.

We wrestled with which monuments, mountain tops, and national parks to stop at and which ones were we willing to forego.

As our trip progressed, we were tempted to bemoan all the things we were missing.

It required a fresh reminder from the Holy Spirit to readjust our focus, *"Enjoy what you **are** getting to see and experience."*

As humans, we tend to swerve into that pitfall of life from time to time, don't we?

We seem to be really good at obsessing over what we *don't* have instead of being grateful for what we *do*.

Ecclesiastes 1:8 sums it up beautifully, *"No matter how much we see, we are never satisfied. No matter how much we hear, we are not content."* (NLT)

That truth can just as easily apply to what we have and don't have, as well.

Whoever coined the popular saying *"The grass is greener on the other side"* clearly put their finger on our human propensity to hone in on and crave what we don't have.

Yielding to this trap quickly robs us of contentment, happiness, and peace.

Choosing to cultivate thankfulness in our lives is the remedy for this snare.

In the book of I Timothy, Paul made this statement, *"Godliness with contentment is a great gain."* (6:6 HCSB)

The context of that verse is nestled in a section speaking about finances; however, the heart of that verse clearly applies to everything in life.

Are you thankful for what you do have today or are you tempted to be preoccupied with all the things you lack?

Nothing can keep our heart as happy as gratefulness can.

> *Reflective Prayer: Father, please cultivate contentedness and thankfulness in my heart. Let me always be grateful for what You have given to me. Amen.*

KEEP YOUR EYES ON JESUS

I sat in my chair and wept.

For days, all I had heard was hard news. Tyranny and human oppression globally, polarizing political agendas nationally, natural catastrophes regionally, and racial tensions locally.

That was heavy enough, but then there were also the personal stories. Precious people I knew who were struggling in their marriages, navigating the challenges of kids who won't listen, or dealing with the heartbreak of tragic loss, sickness, or death in their lives.

On this particular morning, all I could do was cry.

God saw all the needs. He knew all the hurts. He understood all the pain.

Just days before He was hung on a cross, Jesus comforted His disciples with these words, *"Here on earth you will have many trials and sorrows. But take heart, because I have overcome the world."* (John 16:33 NLT)

Heartbreak, tragedy, and suffering is nothing new. These things have been with us since the fall of man.

Being overwhelmed with grief as we weep with those who weep is Scriptural (Romans 12:15), but it's also true that if we don't keep our eyes on Jesus, we'll be tempted to lose heart altogether and spin off into some very dark places.

In the midst of all the chaos, despair, and pain, He's our only hope. He is the only possibility of true joy in such a broken world.

The author of Hebrews knew this and tells us to, *"...lay aside every hindrance (weight, burden) and the sin that so easily ensnares us. Let us run with endurance the race that lies before us,* **keeping our eyes on Jesus***, the source and perfecter of our faith."* (Hebrews 12:1-2 HCSB)

God knew we would need this simple reminder. In a world fraught with dismal circumstances, bad news, and spiritual opposition, it is critical that we learn to keep our eyes on Jesus.

If anyone can sit with you in your heartbreak, it's Him. If anyone can understand the depths of your pain, it's Him. If anyone can comfort you on the deepest of levels, it's Him.

I don't know what form of suffering you're navigating right now, dear friend, but I pray that God will help you fix your eyes on Jesus and be reminded of just how much He loves you and cares for you today.

"God assured us, 'I'll never let you down, never walk off and leave you'..." (Hebrews 13:5 MSG)

> *Reflective Question: Where do I need to shift my focus off of suffering and onto Jesus?*

LETTING GO DOESN'T EQUAL ABANDONMENT

Why is it that we so often question God's love and care for us? Especially when we're in the midst of suffering or the minuses of our day outweigh the pluses.

I remember when my children were little and were learning to ride their bikes. Like most parents, I was there to give them a basic tutorial on how to balance, steer, and brake. I helped them onto the seat, grabbed hold of the bike with both of my hands, and ran beside them as they first learned to pedal and balance.

Then, there came a moment when I would let go. I didn't leave them. I was right there continually watching and ready to help if they needed it. But, in order for them to learn, it was necessary that I let go.

Were there minor crashes? Yes.

Did they get hurt? Only mildly and momentarily.

Did they question my love and care throughout the ups and downs of the process? Not once.

As adults, though, navigating the crashes and falls of life, we tend to work ourselves into a spiritual frenzy thinking God has abandoned us or doesn't care about us because we're experiencing pain (sometimes self-inflicted; sometimes not).

According to the Bible, that's the furthest thing from the truth.

Romans 8:31-38 is a passage that perfectly details how nothing can separate us from God's love, even in the midst of our deepest seasons of suffering.

God knows, as any good parent does, that in order for His kids to grow and learn, they need some space. Sometimes, that space includes the freedom to make mistakes, to fall, and even choose paths that potentially lead to seasons of suffering.

God is in the business of lovingly guiding and helping not controlling.

Can you relate today? Do you feel like God's left you? Doesn't care? Is distant or silent to your pain?

Even Jesus, God's only Son, learned obedience from the things He suffered (Hebrews 5:8).

Whether it's a broken relationship, a dismal medical report, an empty bank account, or anxieties and perplexities that feel suffocating, God is right there.

The pain you're navigating isn't proof that He's abdicated His parental oversight. Quite the contrary. He's inviting you to learn, encouraging you to grow, and cheering you on as you mature in your faith all the while very present to rescue you, if need be.

God let us know ahead of time that we'd experience troubles (sufferings) in this world (John 16:33), but He also promised to never leave us (Hebrews 13:5). That, my friends, is a promise made by Someone who loves us deeply and cares for us without fail.

Whether it's learning to ride a bike or learning to navigate the periodic hardships and sufferings of this life, the principle is the same – God's got this. More importantly, He's got you.

> *Reflective Question: Do I believe that nothing will separate me from God's love today? (Romans 8:35, 38-39)*

LIVING ABUNDANTLY

Once upon a time, I was a single mother. Living paycheck to paycheck was the norm; Ramen noodles was a gourmet meal; and thrift store clothing filled our closets.

Taking care of my children's basic necessities was my sole focus. I didn't have the margin to lavish them with the hottest toys, coolest snacks, or nicest clothes. Our needs were always met. We just didn't have the extra.

It was during this season, though, when God taught us about abundance. Seems contradictory to the natural mind, I know, but with God all things are possible, right?

In John 10:10, Jesus proclaims that He came to give us life. He didn't stop there, though. He went on to add that He would give us *"...life more abundantly."*

So often, American Christianity has interpreted this verse to mean stacks of cash, the finest of clothes, and *Car of the Year's* most trendy vehicle.

But this promise goes so much deeper than the external abundance of possessions.

The abundance Jesus is referring to here is the abundant life that can be found *in Him*. Abundant joy, abundant peace, abundant wisdom, and an abundance of God's Spirit dwelling in us as we believe in Him.

And, herein lies the secret of how a single mother on welfare or a family living below the poverty line can have joy unspeakable and live from a spiritual place that surpasses the amassed prosperity of those on the *Fortune 500's Most Wealthy People in the World* list.

Abundant life comes as we learn there is no worry He cannot carry; no heartache He cannot mend; and no fear He cannot handle.

Yet, how often do we find ourselves acting like He's the God of scarcity? The God of barely enough and meager handouts? The God who has control of the faucet but only turns it on enough to give us a trickle?

Ephesians 3:20 says, *"...to Him who is able to do exceedingly abundantly above all we ask or think..."*

Don't settle for scarcity of peace, joy, or hope today, friend, when we serve a God who came to give us life more abundantly!

Your bank account will never give you that. Doctor's reports can never give you that. The newest, nicest, and best can never give you that.

Only Jesus Christ can give you that.

> *Reflective Prayer: Father, I know that Jesus died so that I may have life and have it more abundantly. Please help me walk in that abundant life today that you promise in your word. Amen.*

MY SHAME IS GONE

I was in a cult once.

No, it was never showcased on an episode of 20/20 or publicized on national news because of its flamboyant and bizarre obedience tactics.

But it was a cult nonetheless and my years spent within it were permeated with harsh mind games, spiritual smoke and mirrors, and an enormous amount of fear.

One of the most common practices of any cult is to ostracize the followers from their family.

Not only were we encouraged to shun our extended families altogether, but there were frequent opportunities for our own nuclear family to be the target of public humiliation and church discipline during weekly meetings.

The result? Wives were pitted against husbands and parents against children as the elders played God with our family dynamics, trust, and loyalty.

Anthony and his proposal of marriage are what set my children and I on a course for deliverance from this destructive group.

However, moving to a new area of the country and starting life over didn't remove the internal shame I carried with me for quite some time.

Shame over things I had said or done towards my confused and concerned parents over the years.

Shame of allowing abusive people access to the lives of my children.

Shame of not leaving this toxic group much earlier than I did.

Shame…shame…shame.

Jesus found me laboring under the weight of it. It took a while for Him to help me unpack all of it and eventually surrender it to Him.

Shame wants us to hide; remain invisible; stay isolated; continue to be tormented. No one has ever been positively changed by the power of shame.

But God, who has deeply loved us from the beginning of time, sent Jesus to die for us. All of our shame, and every bit of our sin, was nailed to the Cross with the Son of God.

"{God} made Christ who knew no sin to be sin on our behalf so that in Him we would become the righteousness of God [that is, we would be made acceptable to Him and placed in a right relationship with Him by His gracious lovingkindness]. (2 Corinthians 5:21 AMP)

Freedom from shame only happens because of that eternal work done on Calvary by Jesus so many years ago.

"…He endured the cross, despising the shame, and sat down at the right hand of the throne of God." (Hebrews 12:2 HCSB)

> *Reflective Prayer: Father, please replace any shame in my life with the forgiveness, grace, mercy, love, hope, and peace that only you can give. Amen.*

NO LOOKING BACK

*Did you sit on **that** bench?*

*Did you eat in **that** restaurant?*

*Did you ever see a movie in **that** theater?*

These (and hundreds more like them) are the types of questions I get asked whenever my husband and I travel back to the area of the country where I was raised. For years, he's exhibited a sincere hunger to want to know every little detail about my past. It makes him feel, to a small degree, like he now shares those particular experiences with me.

Precious, isn't it? It is to me *now*; however, it used to be quite frustrating because I am the extreme opposite.

I don't like looking back. I'm a put-the-pedal-to-the-metal kind of gal. I actively want to move forward; to progress; to advance.

My children tease me on a frequent basis because I seemingly have a crippling inability to recollect events they deem as important. It's in the past. Door closed. Let's move on.

These examples have as much to do with personality differences as anything else.

However, I've also come to the realization more and more as I walk with God that there's not much about my past that I really want to revisit. It's littered with sin, bad choices, and lots of personal carnage. I prefer to look forward knowing that God's sanctifying work in me means the best is *yet to come.*

Paul encouraged some New Testament disciples along the same line. *"One thing I do: forgetting what is behind, I reach forward to what is ahead..."* (Philippians 3:13)

Paul knew what He used to be before God got ahold of him

- a staunch persecutor of Christians and Grade-A Pharisee. He referred to himself later in Scriptures as the "chief of sinners" (I Timothy 1:15). Paul knew what was in his past. He referenced it when it was necessary and helpful but didn't dwell on it.

His testimony became a call to press forward. Move on. Don't look back. The best is *ahead*.

Sure, we all have some memories we could put on a highlight reel that would make us smile (and those are wonderful and should be cherished). But, when it comes to the heart and the work that God is doing in us, let's look forward, forget what is behind, and reach to what is ahead!

Jesus said, "No procrastination. No backward looks...seize the day." (Luke 9:62 MSG)

> *Reflective Question: Are there areas in my life where I need to trust God to help me move forward?*

NOT BY BREAD ALONE

I have a confession. I love bread.

I am one of those strange people in the grocery store who will pick up a loaf of bread just to smell it. It used to embarrass my daughters to no end. Now, they're so used to it, they'll hand me a loaf as we push our buggies through the bread aisle and exclaim, *"Just do it, Mom."*

My love for bread, however, has helped shed some light for me on a statement Jesus made in Matthew 4.

The devil was enticing Jesus to put on a display of His divinity by turning some stones into bread. Jesus responded with, *"...man does not live by bread alone, but by every word that proceeds from the mouth of God."* (vs. 4 NKJV)

I am certain that if I had been the one in that test, I would've found the nearest stash of *Dave's Killer Bread,* grabbed a toaster and a stick of butter, and appeased my longing for carbs.

So, for this bread-loving girl, reading this passage stops me in my tracks every time and reframes my thinking.

Am I being fueled by the word of God today?

Is His word what's nourishing and sustaining me?

Or, am I trying to fill my tank and run on something else?

Those are really the questions for all of us, aren't they?

As people, we tend to replace living by God's word with things – food, relationships, vacations, the news cycle, the list goes on and on.

Options are nearly endless when it comes to things we *think* will satisfy, fuel, or sustain us.

But the truth is, try as I may, no matter how many slices of bread I eat, I eventually wind up hungry again. The gratification I get from eating it is temporary and fleeting.

The gnawing hole returns and begs to be filled.

God's word, on the other hand, is eternal, lasting, tank-filling, and deeply satisfying. It is the one constant in a world offering a variety of shallow substitutions.

"...the word of God is living and active and full of power..." (Hebrews 4:12 AMP)

> *Reflective Question: Am I living by God's word alone or am I trying to be nourished by a substitution?*

NOT TAKING MYSELF TOO SERIOUSLY

Let's just say it was not my finest moment.

We were on vacation in Texas and I (being the photoholic that I am) was itching to get a family picture by the famous San Antonio Riverwalk.

The key was finding a willing stranger who looked like they could do it.

I scanned the crowd on this extremely sunny day and spotted a man sitting on a bench. He had dark glasses on, seemed to be enjoying the sunshine, and appeared to be readily available.

I walked up to him and politely asked if he'd be willing to take our picture.

He smiled, chuckled, and said, *"Ma'am, I don't think you want me taking your picture. I'm blind."*

My face turned a fantastic shade of pink as I apologized (and *then* noticed the white cane with the red tip leaning against his side). Meanwhile, my husband and children stood several feet away stifling their laughter.

Needless to say, I found someone else to take our picture.

But, that embarrassing faux-pas reminded me of a valuable truth – don't take yourself too seriously.

In a world where folks are stressed over being heard, struggling to prove themselves, and jockeying to be seen, I met a blind man with a sense of humor.

He wasn't bitter, he wasn't ashamed, and he didn't convey contempt towards me for asking an inane question.

He smiled and laughed. He didn't take himself too seriously *nor* did his handicap control him.

I wonder how many of us are able to do this?

As human beings, we all have handicaps. It may not be as overt as physical blindness, but we have them. Weaknesses that can tempt us to feel less than, not as important as, or not enough because of.

Paul encourages us to, *"...take pleasure in weaknesses...for the sake of Christ...for when I am weak, then I am strong."* (2 Cor. 12:10 HCSB)

Our weaknesses provide us with a continual reminder that we need Jesus. Every minute of every day.

And, as we embrace our weaknesses and learn not to take ourselves so seriously, we grow in humility, compassion, kindness, and love.

In the words of German theologian Martin Niemoller, *"If you can laugh at yourself, you're going to be fine. If you allow others to laugh with you, you will be great."*

> *Reflective Prayer: Father, please help me laugh often (at myself and life in general) and know that You love me for who I am – weaknesses, handicaps, and hiccups included. Amen.*

PARTICIPATION REQUIRED

Before Anthony and I wed so many years ago, I had reached a point where I thought if God ever wanted me to remarry, He would just bring someone to my door.

Kind of like Amazon home delivery.

God's able to do all things, isn't He? Depositing a marriage candidate on my front porch wasn't beyond His ability, was it?

Laughable, I know.

Because, while God *is* able to do all things, He invites us (and wants us) to participate in what He's doing.

The children of Israel provide a great illustration of this for us. Exodus 16 finds them on their journey through the wilderness, having reached a point where they were hungry and in great need of food.

God told Moses He would supernaturally provide manna – fine flakes that would appear on the ground following the morning dew; however, the people had to actively go out and collect it.

"This is the bread that the Lord has given you to eat...Gather as much of it as each person needs to eat." (Exodus 16:15-16 HCSB)

Participation was required. God supernaturally provided the necessary nourishment, but the people had to actively do something, too – go get it.

How often do we pray and wait for God to show up and do something while taking ourselves out of the equation completely?

How many times do we expect Him to show up like Cinderella's fairy godmother and *"bibbity-bobbity-boo"* wonderful answers into existence for us yet neglect to open His word, connect with Him in prayer, and discern that we usually have a necessary part to play in the answer?

Participation is required.

Following a decade of singleness, I had to actively place myself where I could meet Anthony all those years ago. I had to position myself where I could be seen and found by him.

I had a part to play.

Likewise, God invites us into action today. Many times, the answers to our prayers involve some obedient legwork on our part.

God always promises to do His part. The question is, are we doing ours?

> *Reflective Question: Am I actively posturing myself today to participate with God in what He's doing in my life?*

RELATIONSHIP > RELIGION

I have never been a big fan of religion. The word alone evokes thoughts of formality, rituals, and emptiness to me. I spent a good chunk of my life entrenched in religion and I never saw it avail any good.

When my heart has been most broken, my emotions most raw, and my soul most vulnerable, religion has done nothing to help me.

But Jesus has.

His life, His story, and the way He continually interacts with us is the exact opposite of religion. He's real, vulnerable, sincere and consistently *relational.*

John 21 highlights a story that is such a perfect example of this.

Jesus had already been crucified and resurrected. A few of His disciples, still suffering from the shellshock of recent events and crushed with discouragement, decided to go fishing.

Following an unsuccessful night in their boat, Jesus appeared to them and told them to toss their nets back in the water. The result was a haul of fish so large that they could barely drag the full net in.

Once they did, though, Jesus (who already had a fire ready on the beach) told them to bring some of the fish over and *"Come and have breakfast."* (vs. 12)

Is there anything more genuinely human and relational than that? No formality here. Just grab a seat and let's eat! He didn't chastise them for their recent bout with discouragement or browbeat them with any hoops to jump through to ensure His favor.

Nope. He just wanted to sit with these fellas and enjoy some food and conversation together. They were friends. He wanted that relationship with them.

It's so raw, isn't it?! There's nothing polished or sterile about it. If you pause and take a minute, you can almost feel the sand, hear the water lapping on the shore, and smell the smoke from the fire.

Religion tends to keep people at arm's length. Shrouded in mystery and confusion, it doesn't offer much help when you're picking up the pieces of a broken marriage, the medical reports are touch-and-go, or the weight of your daily stress pulls your mind into some very dark places.

But Jesus invites us to come close to Him – have a seat, be in His presence, and talk about what's on our mind as He promises to walk alongside us through life with all of its ups and downs.

> *Reflective Prayer: Father, help me experience the enjoyment of Your company today knowing that You are a real friend who sticks closer than a brother (Proverbs 18:24) and that You deeply enjoy having a relationship with me. Amen.*

SEEING PIECES OF HIS HEART

It happens every time I fly.

Without exception, my husband will track me. He pulls up a website where you can see all the airline flights of the day, punches in my flight number, and watches me from wheels-up to wheels-down.

Endearing, isn't it?

It is to me now, but during the first several years of our marriage, It used to irritate me to no end.

Having taken care of myself for so long before Anthony and I got married, my immediate thought was he didn't trust me.

Why else would he have reason to stalk...I mean, track my every move?

The idea that he was watching over me because he *cared* for me didn't even enter my mind.

It was a blind spot God knew I had from years of being on my own. A hard, self-protective layer over my heart that I didn't even know existed.

And, over the years, God has used this small, consistent act of Anthony's to soften and reshape my heart (and mind) to better understand *His constant care* for me.

Maybe you can relate.

It may not be an airplane-tracking husband. It might be a prayer warrior of a parent or a kind-hearted co-worker, a generous neighbor or a friend who's quick to forgive.

God will often use other people in our lives to reveal and demonstrate pieces of His divine heart and character that we need to see most.

The process happens over time.

Their steadfast example helps shine a light on Christlike traits (mercy, care, kindness, love, forgiveness, etc.) that God is using to mold us into His image even further.

"Imitate me, as I imitate Christ," Paul said in I Corinthians 11:1.

Who can you credit today for imitating Christlike behavior to you?

For me, I never take to the skies now without thinking about how much God cares for me.

Because of Anthony.

> *Reflective Question: How can I show someone a piece of God's heart today?*

SOARING LIKE A...TURKEY

I saw him as he was running towards the road. A turkey, in a frantic effort to launch himself into the air, came within mere inches of my windshield before gaining enough upward momentum to clear it.

While this event happened in a split second, it felt like the turkey and I were locked in a slo-mo scene from a movie.

His running motion was labored and looked more like a disjointed wobble. His lift-off was awkward and cumbersome as his pudgy body listed from side to side. His mouth was wide open and looked like he was trying to holler, *"Clear the runway!"* to the rest of the world.

The image was almost cartoonish. I smiled as I continued driving down the road and thought to myself, "Poor thing, he was *really* trying to fly."

Fly he did, though. Granted, it wasn't for long and he didn't go very high. But, he flew! Sure, somewhere in the forest, a hawk was probably rolling his eyes, but that turkey flew!

I don't know about you, but there are many days when I can relate to this turkey. Days when it barely feels like I'm getting my feet off the ground. I want to soar, but it just isn't happening.

Ever had those days? Days where you sleep through your morning alarm? Days where your children have more energy than you have caffeine? Days where your car keys are playing hide-and-seek as your list of errands and appointments calls your name?

I have good news, friends!

God promises to help us soar like eagles as we lean on Him.

One of my favorite Bible verses comes from Isaiah 40. *"He [God] gives strength to the faint and strengthens the powerless...those who trust in the Lord will renew their strength; they will soar on wings like eagles..."* (vs. 29 & 31)

While I'm not an expert in fowl flights, flapping, or fluttering, I can attest that God's word is true and He is faithful. I've also witnessed eagles in the air and there's almost nothing more majestic and graceful. They clearly have air navigation mastered as they soar to heights that other birds only dream of.

If you feel like your day is in "turkey mode," take a minute and ask God to strengthen you like an eagle. Better than anyone else, He can teach you to lift off, strengthen you to fly, and sustain you as you soar!

Reflective Prayer: Father, please strengthen me with Your power and might, renew my strength and hope today, and help me to soar like an eagle as I put my trust in You. Amen.

SOMETIMES LOVE ISN'T CONVENIENT

My daughter and I had to do a double-take.

Did we just pass a body near the side of the road?

Within a matter of seconds, I had turned the car around.

There, lying on the side of the road with his head inches from the pavement, was a man. I parked my car and ran towards him while my daughter immediately called 911.

Traffic started to back-up and our plans were abruptly put on pause.

As I reached him, it was apparent that he was conscious and didn't appear to be hurt. When I looked into his eyes, I knew immediately what the problem was.

Alzheimer's.

The far-away, lost, and disconnected gaze quickly spoke volumes to me about how this man had probably wandered from his home, walked down the street, and fallen along the side of this busy road.

Having spent countless hours with my mother, who battled this terrifying disease for a decade before passing away, I became all too familiar with the look, the mannerisms, and the consuming darkness of this sickness.

By this point, traffic had completely backed-up in both directions. Tucked comfortably in their cars, people grew impatient. Horns honked and tempers flared as I walked this man across the road to get him back to his home and wait for first responders to arrive.

I sympathized. There have been plenty of times when I've driven up on the scene of an accident or an emergency and had my life suddenly "backed-up" because of the interruption. My schedule put on hold. My time frame inconvenienced.

The truth is, loving our neighbor isn't always convenient. Helping that person in need doesn't always fit neatly into our daily planners.

It wasn't convenient for the Good Samaritan who adjusted his own journey in order to help a complete stranger (Luke 10:30-35).

It certainly wasn't convenient for Jesus when He hung on a cross – bloodied and battered – to save us.

Simply stated, love isn't about convenience, it's about choices. Small, minute by minute, daily choices to do for others what we want and hope they would do for us (Luke 6:31).

> *Reflective Question: How might God be calling me to love in an "inconvenient" way today?*

STOP THE BLEED

My foot was turning purple.

I looked around the room. The other participants were wincing and squirming as much as I was.

All of us volunteered to come to this emergency response class but judging by the distraught looks and vehement moans coming from everyone in the room, I was fairly certain folks were secretly wishing they had just stayed home to watch TV right about now.

I was beyond thrilled when the instructor told us we could remove our tourniquets.

Yes, tourniquets.

As part of the "Stop the Bleed" class, this exercise had been necessary. It was important to "feel" just how tight a tourniquet should be. If we were ever in a situation where we'd need to actually apply one to help save a person's life, we had this first-hand experience to draw from.

As the color began to return to our limbs and our class sat back in relief, the instructor said these profound words, "It's important to know that if you ever need to do this in a real-life situation, the person will fight you. *You will need to work against the person in order to save their life.*"

WHOA.

As the weight of those words sunk in, I thought of Paul.

Known forever as the man who wrote more than half of the New Testament, Paul did not start off as God's friend. It took an eye-opening, knock-down encounter with God to stop the internal spiritual bleeding in Paul and, ultimately, save his life.

Paul had been busy ravaging the church, throwing Christ-followers in prison and even went as far as killing some (Acts 8:1-3).

Acts 9:1 tells us he was, *"breathing threats and murder against the disciples of the Lord."*

Until, God confronted Paul one day and asked him, *"...why are you persecuting Me? It is useless for you to fight against My will."* (Acts 26:14 NLT)

This "stop the bleed" moment for Paul was the life-saving intervention he needed. Prior to this, Paul had been religiously running amok, squandering precious time, and resisting his ultimate purpose to love God and follow Jesus.

It took this tourniquet moment from God to give Paul a second chance and a new life.

While we may not be exhibiting such extreme outward behavior as Paul did, we all still have wounds that require life-saving measures.

The question is, are we fighting against God or cooperating with Him?

It's not going to "feel good" as God begins working in an area of our life that needs intervention – it may be an unhealthy habit, addiction, or relationship. It's painful and our natural reaction will be to fight against Him.

Yet, just like the "Stop the Bleed" class taught me, that is counterintuitive. We need to remember that the pain tends to increase momentarily before the healing can begin.

I don't know about you, but I am so grateful to Jesus for the countless times He's worked *against* me for my good!

> *Reflective Prayer: Father, thank You for stopping the bleed in me and giving me a second chance to live. Let everything I do and say bring You glory – today, tomorrow, and forever.*

THE ACT OF IMITATING

Eyewitnesses to the account say I was three. I have no memory of it personally.

In the early 70's, my family shared a two-story house with my grandparents – grandma and grandpa lived on the ground level; dad, mom, and I on the top.

This particular day I had sauntered downstairs while my grandma was getting food ready for dinner. Part of her prep work entailed piercing a piece of meat repeatedly so that it could cook thoroughly.

I adored my grandma and typically wanted to do everything she did. So, I found myself a random pencil and the nearest hassock and began to stab away as I copied the action I saw her performing.

As the story goes, I was profusely scolded. I have no memory of that, either (And, for those of you tender-hearted souls who may be wondering – yes, the hassock survived).

I guarantee there's not a person reading this who doesn't understand the principle of that story. The act of learning by example or copying someone's behavior or traits that we admire is as old as humanity itself.

As I grew, I helped my grandma in the kitchen, watched and followed her example, and used some of her recipes. In doing so, I became more accomplished and developed in my cooking and baking skills until I could replicate some of the dishes she served (I am still nowhere near my grandma's skill level, but progress has occurred!).

It took time. It didn't happen overnight. It was a process of patience, persistence, and growth.

Just like following Jesus. While choosing to be born again and giving Jesus the steering wheel of your life is instantaneous, the process of growing, maturing, and developing in Him takes time to unfold.

Paul had a great understanding of this. He told the newly converted Christians of the Corinthian church to *"imitate me, as I also imitate Christ."* (I Cor. 11:1 HCSB)

That foundational truth still applies to us today. Regardless of where you find yourself in your Christian journey, imitating Christ is always our daily goal.

Are we looking more like Him today? Are we acting more like Him today? Does our speech sound more like Him today?

"...be imitators of God, as dearly loved children." (Eph. 5:1 HCSB)

> *Reflective Prayer: Father, please help me imitate You today –*
> *I want to reflect Your heart, mirror Your behavior, and speak*
> *in such a manner that points others to You. Amen.*

THE PRICE OF FRIENDSHIP

My bill came to $4.44.

A small price to invest in fostering a friendship, I thought.

I had just enjoyed a delicious cup of coffee while spending the last hour engaged in lively conversation with a dear friend. We wrapped up our time together with a bear hug and parted ways with big smiles and full hearts.

I looked down again at my receipt and smiled. It was worth every penny and more!

We invest in what we love, don't we? We pour time, energy, and money into pursuing things that are close to our hearts.

Yet, how often do we foster our friendships with this truth in mind?

"A sweet friendship refreshes the soul." (Proverbs 27:9)

God didn't create us to do life alone. We were made for community, fellowship, and belonging. Our weary souls need the company of precious friends as we navigate this temporary life.

But, as the world becomes more cynical than ever and trust in our fellow man plummets to all-time lows, the temptation to isolate ourselves is very real.

The Scripture highlights the danger in that, however. *"One who isolates himself pursues selfish desires; he rebels against all sound wisdom."* (Proverbs 18:1 CSB)

Jesus didn't die on the cross so we could look like the world.

Or be isolated.

He showed us the value of friendships and doing life together as He handpicked 12 guys that would be His closest confidants during His life here on earth.

He modeled how to cultivate those friendships including how to be vulnerable and let people "in" even at the risk of getting hurt or being betrayed (check out the story of Judas).

His friends did life with Him, prayed with Him, shared meals with Him, and provided community for Him. And, like Jesus, we were made to need friends.

The price of a cup of coffee or a lunch is so small compared to the benefit and blessing of having people who are there for you, love you, and care enough about you to encourage you!

The true value of friendship is priceless but every $4.44 helps!

Reflective Prayer: Father, thank You for the friends You have blessed me with! Please help me cherish and foster those relationships in ways that glorify You and reflect Your heart and love to others. Amen.

TRASH BAGS OF TEDDY BEARS

Have you ever had God show up and take care of something before you even had the chance to ask Him to?

It was one of the most broken and fragile seasons of my life.

I was a young, single mother. My divorce had not only shattered the stability of our family but it also stripped me of any real financial security.

My husband had been the breadwinner in our marriage. Suddenly, I found myself wondering how I was going to pay the bills, buy food, and put gas in my car.

A friend at the time, knowing my dire circumstances, gave me a piece of paper with a telephone number on it. It was to a company not far from where I was living that assembled teddy bears.

The company would cut the teddy bear patterns from huge bolts of brown, fuzzy cloth. Then, they would hire local folks to take these cut-outs home and sew them together. For every bear returned, the sewer got fifty cents.

I called the number, expressed my interest, and within a few days my children and I picked up as many trash bags full of pre-cut bears as we could stuff into my used Nissan hatchback.

Once home, I sat down at my antique sewing machine and worked into the wee hours of the morning. My goal was to return each load of bears as fast as I could to make as much money as I was able in order to take care of my children.

During that season, the verse in Matthew 6 became very real to me, *"...your Father knows the things you need before you ask Him."* (vs. 8)

God knew my bills needed paid. He knew I needed to buy groceries. He knew my car needed gas. And, He provided – before I even had the chance to talk to Him about it.

Over the years, I've shared this story with several people to fan the flame of faith. When things seem the most bleak, He shows up (many times before we even ask). When circumstances seem the most hopeless, He provides.

Where have you seen God show up in your life? How have you seen Him provide for you?

The most profound testimony of God's character we have comes from our own personal experiences.

Sharing our stories with others helps to make Jesus real – alive and active, close and personal. This not only rekindles our faith but helps activate it in those we share our stories with.

"Lord my God, you have done many…wondrous works…more than can be told." (Psalm 40:5)

> *Reflective Question: Is there a piece of my God-story that I can share with someone today to help them see Jesus more clearly?*

UNSANITIZED PRAYERS

Have you ever felt like there are just some things you can't say to God? Or that when you do talk to Him, you somehow need to put your words into a holy sentence structure?

As a young Christ-follower, I sure did. I was convinced that if I didn't polish my words and pray with certain religious verbiage, God wouldn't listen.

Nothing could be further from the truth.

If you can't be raw, unfiltered, and completely vulnerable with God, then who can you be that way with?

David, referred to as *"a man after God's own heart"* in Acts 13:22, is one of the best examples of this.

David's walk with God had more ups and downs, twists and turns than the world's best roller-coaster.

He defeated Goliath, became one of Israel's most well-known kings, committed adultery with Bathsheba, had her husband murdered, and embarked on an abundance of other exploits to numerous to name here.

With the highs and lows of his life documented for all of us to study, the way he prays should not be overlooked.

A huge chunk of the Psalms were written by David. As you read through them, you'll notice they are basically a collection of unsanitized prayers.

David removes any religion from his conversations with God and just tells it like it is. He says what he means, describes what he's feeling, and pours out his every raw emotion.

David knew it was foolish to try and sanitize his words. What would be the point? Didn't God already see and know everything about him? Was there anything David had already said or done that God had not been privy to (Psalm 139:1-5)?

The same is true for us today.

God *wants* us to talk to Him – unfiltered; unsanitized; completely raw.

He already sees your anger, worry, frustration, and bitterness. He already knows about that sin, that secret, that addiction, that heartbreak.

There are no special words, phrases, or flowery church jargon that God is looking for. He just wants you – the real you – to talk to Him. Dump out the hurt, the pain, the anxiety, the fear...in your own words.

Don't hold back. David didn't. He brought his authentic, broken, and very real self to his conversations with God, was called *a man after God's own heart,* and saw God move in his life in some incredible ways!

> *Reflective Question: How can I be more authentic and real with God in prayer?*

VICTORIOUS CHIPPING

I heard him before I saw him.

Tick, tick, tick, tick.

I continued walking about my yard enjoying the calm of the early morning.

Tick, tick, tick, tick.

I stopped. My eyes searched for the source of the noise that hit my soul like a jackhammer on this tranquil start to a new day.

I finally spotted him. The smallest of woodpeckers sitting on a tremendously thick tree branch.

His little head was moving at the speed of light as he hammered away fiercely.

This tiny fellow was clearly just beginning his young woodpecker life and hadn't been schooled yet on the topic of *"This Branch is Too Thick for You."*

I giggled as I watched him. I also wondered if he really thought he was making any progress. Would he eventually realize his efforts were futile? Would Mom or Dad Woodpecker appear and redirect him to a branch that would be better suited for Junior?

In spite of those thoughts, though, I was internally cheering him on.

Because, in my heart, I desire to see the underdog win.

If we're being honest, we all do, don't we?

That's why people make movies about David and Goliath type stories or write books about down-and-out sports teams that rise to great victories against all odds.

It resonates with us because we have all been the underdog at some point in our life. We have all faced circumstances or challenges that just seemed far too great for us.

It's why the Gospel hits our heart and soul so squarely. Jesus willingly chose to position Himself against **all** odds. He appeared overwhelmed, outnumbered, and tremendously insignificant and weak.

We cheer when we read "the end" of His story and learn of the eternal victory He secured for us. He overcame the most impossible of circumstances and purposefully set the stage for us to be overcomers like He was.

"For everyone born of God is victorious and overcomes the world..." (I John 5:4 AMP)

And, while that promise is definitively true, some challenges take time. Not all obstacles can be overcome instantaneously. Hammering away might be required.

Whether it's continuing to chip away on that new diet and lifestyle changes you've made to become healthier or undoing wrong thinking and bad habits from your past, some challenges require time, patience, and dedication in order to overcome.

But, overcoming is guaranteed. Victory is certain for the one willing to keep chipping away. Triumph, against all odds, is promised.

"...thanks be to God, who gives us the victory through our Lord Jesus Christ!" (I Cor. 15:57 HCSB)

Reflective Question: What is God encouraging me to keep chipping away at today?

WALKING EACH OTHER HOME

While browsing the aisles of a boutique, I spotted it. A small piece of home décor. Circular and wooden with a neatly tied white cord attached so as to hang it on a wall. Painted on it the words, *"We're all just walking each other home."*

The statement penetrated my heart and my eyes became damp as this simple message resonated with my soul.

Each of us finds ourself on a journey as we navigate life on this earth...and, none of us are called to walk it alone.

For those whose hope is found in Christ, we understand that the earth is not our home. All the trials, sorrows, and pain of this physical life are just passing, fleeting, and temporary.

Hebrews 11 is often referred to as the "faith chapter" because it's packed full of examples of men and women who hung on tightly to a heavenly God while walking through this temporary life of challenges and hardships on earth.

*"...they confessed that they were **foreigners and temporary residents on the earth**...those who say such things make it clear that **they are seeking a homeland**."* (Hebrews 11:13 & 14 – emphasis mine)

They knew earth was just a passing through point. They also understood the value and necessity of helping other sojourners on the way.

"Carry one another's burdens; in this way you will fulfill the law of Christ." (Galatians 6:2)

For years, every time I read that verse, I would picture a couple traveler's helping each other with their loads. Sharing the weight of what's in their backpacks. Stopping when one gets winded and needs a break.

The spiritual application of this is a constant as we journey together towards eternity. This life can be hard, tiring, and wearisome. We need each other. It's more than just a suggestion; it's a divine instruction so as to fully demonstrate the love of God.

Who do you know that is carrying a burden that you can help shoulder? Perhaps it's as simple as texting that person to let them know you care and are praying for them today.

How can you lighten the load of that friend who is carrying the weight of a troubling medical diagnosis or a strained marriage? Sometimes just an invitation to coffee where you offer your gift of time and a listening ear does wonders to a friend's soul who feels alone, scared, and isolated.

Remember, we're all just walking each other home. Who can you help along the way today?

> *Reflective Prayer: Father, open my eyes to see the unique ways that I can actively help someone today. Help me to love and care in a way that helps others know they are not walking alone. Amen.*

WEAR YOUR OWN ARMOR

It wasn't working and my frustration was mounting.

I was a relatively young Christian in my faith journey and a fellow believer had shared with me about how they had prayed and God had answered.

Excitedly, I probed them with all sorts of questions concerning their prayer time so I could duplicate the process in hopes of getting some answers myself.

Then, I scurried off to pray.

But, it wasn't working. The only thing I took away from *my* "time with God" was discouragement and perplexity.

It took me months before I realized I was trying to wear another person's armor.

And I wasn't the first...

I Samuel 17 shares a story with us about David going into battle against the giant Goliath. As this teenage shepherd boy was gearing up to head onto the battlefield in a solo match against this killing machine, Israel's King Saul offered David his personal armor.

After putting the pieces on and walking around in them, David announced, *"I can't walk in these. I'm not used to them."* (vs. 39)

David took them off. *"Instead, he took his staff in his hand and chose five smooth stones from the wadi and put them...in his shepherd's bag."* (vs. 40)

David defeated Goliath that day, ushering in a huge victory for Israel. But, David did it in a way that "fit" him. He wore his shepherd's clothing and used his sling and his stones.

You see, he was a shepherd boy, not a military man. Slings and stones were the weapons he was familiar with as he used them regularly to keep his flocks safe against predators. The heavy, military armor was unfamiliar, awkward, and cumbersome to him.

My personal "a-ha!" moment came as I applied this story to my prayer life and spiritual walk. Copying someone else's prayer style, habits, and ways had been mechanical to me and burdensome because it didn't *fit me*.

God wasn't as concerned about where I prayed, how I prayed, and what I was wearing when I prayed as much as He was about my heart. Was I being authentic? Genuine? Transparent and real? Was I being true to myself – to come to Him in ways that fit how He made me?

I'm a chatterbox and pray best when I can move. It helps me think, be expressive, and connect with God deeply. For others, sitting still or walking a nature trail works best.

Whatever the case may be, we each have a unique way that reflects how we best connect with God as we step onto our spiritual battlefields daily.

Admiring someone else's prayer life, spiritual walk, or gifts and talents is one thing; trying to outwardly duplicate their actions will only tend to cause agonizing disappointment.

> *Reflective Prayer: Father, please help me wear my own armor, be who You've made me to be, and not try to be anyone else. Amen.*

WHEN A SEAL TAUGHT ME ABOUT CARE

It happens without any effort (or permission) on my part.

Every time I thank a veteran for their service, my emotions think they need to be involved.

I'm not sure why. It may be because my Dad served in Vietnam. It may be because I feel so deeply about anyone voluntarily signing up to (potentially) lay down their life to protect mine.

Whatever the reason, it always happens. A lump wells up in my throat, my voice shakes and my eyes get misty.

However, my emotional display was elevated to a whole new level when I came face to face with a former Navy Seal.

I had just finished listening to this man's hour-long breakout session during a leadership conference. His presentation overflowed with fascinating tales and incredible pictures from his Navy Seal days.

Afterwards, I stood in a small book-signing line to meet him.

My mind was working to give my emotions a stabilizing pep-talk as my internal dialogue went something like this: *"Now when you meet him, just look him in the eye, shake his hand, and tell him thank you. Hold it together, Kristen…there's no need to cry…"*

When my turn arrived, I walked up to him, looked him squarely in the eyes, firmly shook his hand…and started to fall apart.

My voice quivered, eroded, and finally collapsed into broken words as I desperately tried to convey my thanks for his military service while choking back tears.

He got up from his seat, came around the book-signing table, and asked me a question, "Can I give you a hug?"

That did it. The ripcord had been pulled and I was freefalling into a complete ugly cry as I hugged this Navy Seal I'd never met before.

While people around us turned to see what the commotion was about, this man looked at me and used this awkward moment to do something I didn't see coming.

He thanked me for caring.

Care. It's the very thread that holds the fabric of humanity together, isn't it?

It's why people enlist in the military.

It's why parents lose sleep.

It's why doctors and nurses cry when their shift is over.

It's why Jesus went to the cross.

Care drives us to love, to serve, and to lay down our lives for others. (John 15:13)

> *Reflective Question: How can I show someone in my life a little extra care today?*

WHEN I LEAST EXPECTED IT

It's one of my favorite stories to tell. How Anthony and I met.

Back when internet dating sites were just becoming a thing, I shared a home with another single mom (this convenient arrangement helped us pay the bills and provided in-home childcare for both of us).

Desperate to be married, my housemate quickly jumped on several of these new dating sites and posted complete profiles that included the best pictures of herself she could find, hobbies that sounded fun and interesting, and detailed some specifics of what she was looking for in a future mate.

She repeatedly encouraged, i.e., hounded me to jump online and try it, too.

No thanks. Not for me. I was very content in my singleness.

Months went by and she hadn't relented. So, when one of these sites offered a two-week free trial membership (because there was *no way* I was going to *pay* for this foolishness), I acquiesced.

I intentionally posted a picture that would scare away mice (not attract men) and offered as little in the "description" category as possible.

The profile went "live" and the countdown began.

Four days in, Anthony sent me a message. The rest, as they say, is history.

Obviously, there is *a lot* more to this story; however, the element that strikes me every time I share it is how God will show up when we least expect it.

I wasn't looking for a husband. Truth be told, I didn't even want to be married. I did everything in my power when I posted that profile to ensure no one would be remotely interested in me.

But God showed up. In a way I least expected. At a time I least expected.

It was all God, no Kristen.

"...the way I work surpasses the way you work, and the way I think is beyond what you think." (Isaiah 55:9 MSG)

Not only did God show up when I least expected it, but He clearly knew what I needed even more than I did.

I cannot imagine my life without Anthony now and wouldn't have ever dreamed of learning, growing, and being sanctified these past couple decades together in ways that God clearly knew I would cherish and need.

Reflective Question: Have you ever seen God show up when you've least expected it? Take a moment and just thank Him for those times.

WHITE SPACE

As a writer, I value white space – those wonderful areas on the page that are free of type and give room for the eyes to easily read the author's words in an orderly fashion. Without this precious space, the page would be chaotic, jumbled, and overwhelming.

White space isn't just limited to authors, though. It also applies to our calendars and our personal lives.

How many of us live without white space? We dash from one thing to the next, fall into bed exhausted, and wake still feeling drained and wonder why.

Our calendars are filled from sun-up to sun-down with appointments, meetings, and activities leaving no margin for thought and reflection, quiet, or quality time with God.

I've walked through plenty of seasons in my life where I neglected this space and burned the candle at both ends. I didn't like who I became in those seasons either – stressed, edgy, irritable, and drained. One of the walking dead in the land of the living.

Those mind-numbing, energy-zapping seasons helped me deeply understand the need for white space, boundaries, and intentionally carving out time in my daily and weekly rhythms for me.

On the surface, it can sound selfish, I know. But when you dig deep and begin incorporating white space into your life, you begin to realize that the healthier you are, the happier you are and the better positioned you are to help others.

People are people, regardless of their careers, faith, or family connections. It seems we have a universal tendency to view unsustainable busyness as some sort of badge of honor (even though it's been scientifically proven that, over time, it takes a steep toll on our mental, physical, and emotional health).

Recognizing our limits, coming to terms with our humanity, and beginning to block off designated chunks of white space into our schedules is something God always knew we would need. He made us that way – to be dependent, weak, finite, needing time off, sleep, pockets of rest, and seasons to recharge.

"Be still, and know that I am God..." (Psalm 46:10)

Be still.

Take a break. It's ok – the world will keep spinning and life will go on. It will still be here when you plug back in.

Christian pastor and author Wayne Cordeiro aptly sums it up, *"Rest has to be a primary responsibility. It brings a rhythm back to life and a cadence that makes life sustainable."*

> *Reflective Question: Do I have white space on my calendar? Margins that are blank and open just for me to be rejuvenated?*

WORKOUTS WITH HERSHEY

I've come to a point in my life where I've learned a few foundationally helpful things - feelings are fickle, hair *does* grow back, and sometimes it's okay to eat chocolate on the treadmill.

It's true! Because as much as I'd like them to be, not every day is a red letter day.

There are days when I'm raring to go and I jump on my treadmill like I'm training for the Olympics. But, there are also days when a few Hershey's kisses are my companion as I step onto what feels like a conveyor belt taking me nowhere.

In both cases, I show up, do the work and get on the treadmill. It just doesn't feel as easy some days (thus, the morsels of chocolate motivation).

Recently, during one of these workouts with Hershey, I was thinking about Paul's encouragement to Timothy to be faithful *"in season and out of season."* The context was Timothy's ministry.

"Preach the word; be ready in season and out of season; rebuke, correct, and encourage with great patience and teaching." (2 Timothy 4:2)

Paul knew that Timothy wouldn't always feel like fulfilling his calling.

Timothy was only human. His enthusiasm to preach, teach, and encourage would certainly ebb and flow as he encountered good days and bad - days when the Lord felt near and days when it seemed like He was nowhere to be found.

Adding to that was the culture during Timothy's days. People were turning away from sound doctrine as they surrounded themselves with a myriad of teachers because they had *"an itch to hear what they wanted to hear."* (vs. 3&4)

Paul understood that Timothy would be swimming upstream and would need this added encouragement to be ready in season and out of season – because of his flesh, society's increased ungodliness, and, of course, the enemy.

So, how does this apply to us today?

We will not feel "on fire" for Jesus every day of this life – our flesh will get in the way and the godless voices of our culture will pull for our attention.

Weariness and worldliness can set in if we're not vigilant.

But, like Timothy, we have a purpose, mission, and calling to walk out our God-given purpose – *in season and out of season* – regardless of convenience and our feelings.

> *Reflective Prayer: Father, please help me show up today as I persist and persevere where You've called me. Remind me of my eternal purpose and use me for Your glory! Amen.*

WORSHIP 24/7

There I was, sitting in the extremely cushy spa chair. A very sweet lady kindly worked away on my pedicure while I completely relaxed and sunk into this moment of self-care.

As I flipped through the color book trying to decide on which shade of pink polish to get, I worshipped.

(Perhaps you're scratching your head and thinking, *"Wait... what??"*)

The truth is, we don't tend to equate getting our nails done as an act of worship, do we?

For most, the word worship evokes thoughts of church attendance and singing hymns or praise songs to God.

And while both of those things are absolutely true, I would challenge us to go even deeper than that.

By relegating worship to *just* a Sunday morning experience, we really limit our application of what God intends true worship to be.

The simple dictionary definition of worship is "to show reverence and adoration for God."

As Christ-followers, don't we do that just by being alive? Aren't our transformed lives an expression of worship every minute of every day?

Romans 12:1 says it this way, *"...I urge you to present your bodies as a living sacrifice, holy and pleasing to God; this is your true worship."* (HCSB)

Elsewhere, the Scriptures say, *"...whether you eat or drink, or whatever you do, do all to the glory of God."* (I Corinthians 10:31 ESV)

Whatever you do...

Sitting at the park during a lunchbreak = worship.

Playing with your kids = worship.

Enjoying some date time with your spouse = worship.

Spending quality time with great friends = worship.

Walking next door to meet the new neighbors = worship.

Taking some time for self-care = worship.

Sleeping at night = worship.

See the pattern?

Everything – every breath, word, and action – is worship because, as Christ-followers, we are saying or doing those things to ultimately glorify God!

We are living, breathing vessels that have come alive by the Spirit of God. Our lives are now on display as an unbroken act of worship (Ephesians 2:1-10)!

Sometimes, in religious circles especially, we can get derailed thinking worship is a special act or work. That we need to have a certain feeling or be in a specific posture.

Not true.

Jesus gave us an incredible example to follow. He modeled a life of worship for us – every minute of His day was poured out as a living sacrifice in reverence and adoration to His Father.

Whether He was having dinner at a stranger's house, speaking to thousands from a hilltop, attending a wedding, or hanging out at the beach with His friends, His life was worship 24/7.

He was worshipping just by being alive!

So. Are. You.

> *Reflective Question: Am I viewing my very existence as an act of worship to God?*

YOU ARE NOT ALONE

Are you on a faith journey?

If so, here's a little spoiler alert – there will be countless times when you feel like you're walking the path *alone*.

For the last 35 years of my life, I have been journeying with Jesus. Much of that time has been spent surrounded by people that love me, care for me, and have "been there" for me.

But, when God has called me to pick up my cross (navigating divorce, blending a family, dealing with the shadows of my past, and various other this-doesn't-feel-good moments), it tends to be in a very personal and isolated kind of way.

Hours before Jesus was crucified, He had been praying in a garden with three of His closest friends. The burden of the next 24-hours was weighing heavily upon Him. The expectation of betrayal, abuse, and a violent execution had Jesus sweating blood.

It was about to be His darkest hour.

The Gospel of Mark gives us a snapshot as to the level of support Jesus received from His family and friends at this time.

"Then they all deserted Him and ran away." (Mark 14:50)

He was alone.

As Christ-followers, we all face moments, seasons, and circumstances in our lives when it looks like we've been abandoned and deserted by others. It feels like we're facing the dark by ourselves.

And, from a human standpoint, we are.

No one else can really understand what it feels like to navigate the pain of your miscarriage, the devastation of that trauma or addiction, or that difficult medical diagnosis you received. No one else can truly feel the weight of your broken marriage or prodigal child.

Sure, friends can empathize; family can support; the church can pray. But, only you can walk the path. It can (and will) feel very, very lonely.

Jesus knew what it felt like to suffer and be alone.

The good news is that we never are. His promise from Hebrews 13:5 that He'll *"never leave us or forsake us"* remains true *and*, following His resurrection, He even left us with the gift of the Holy Spirit (also called the "Comforter" in John 14:26)!

Are you feeling alone today, friend? Isolated and like no one understands what you're going through?

May I introduce you to the One who never has abandoned you? Let Him comfort and strengthen you today.

He sees you. He loves you. He is with you.

> *Reflective Prayer: Father, I ask for comfort and peace. Please help me remember that You never leave me even when others do. Help me rest in this truth today. Amen.*

ABOUT THE AUTHOR

Kristen West

Kristen West is a communicator who is passionate about inspiring, encouraging, and challenging others in their walk with Christ. With light-hearted humor and refreshing transparency, her writing highlights what God has done in her life so that others may find that same hope in theirs.

She and her husband Anthony live in the Northwest Georgia area of the Blue Ridge Mountains and are empty-nesters. In addition to writing, she loves to spend time with her grown children, curl up with insightful books, and travel just about anywhere (especially if coffee is involved)!

Follow and connect with Kristen by going to kristen-west.com.

Made in the USA
Columbia, SC
18 August 2024